Jazz Saxophone Duets
Volume 2

by Greg Fishman

Published by Greg Fishman Jazz Studios
Evanston, Illinois 60202

ISBN: 978-0-9843492-0-3
©2010 Greg Fishman

All rights reserved. International copyright secured. No part of this book or CD set may be reproduced or transmitted in any form or by any means, electronic or mechanical, including photocopying or recording, or by any information storage and retrieval system, without permission in writing from the publisher. Violation of copyright is subject to all applicable laws.

Published by Greg Fishman Jazz Studios
824 Custer Avenue, Evanston, Illinois 60202
www.gregfishmanjazzstudios.com
greg@gregfishmanjazzstudios.com

Jazz Saxophone
Volume 2
Table of Contents

Preface…………………………………………………………………....	4
Credits…………………………………………………………………..	5
Suggested Use of This Book and CD Set………………………….	7
Style and Analysis…………………………………………………….	13
Detailed Overview of the Etudes……………………………………	15

Duets for Two Altos or Two Tenors:

Fairbanks Court……………………………………………………...	16
Armitage Avenue…………………………………………………….	18
Ozark Avenue………………………………………………………...	20
Peterson Avenue…………………………………………………….	22
Wilson Avenue……………………………………………………….	24
Belle Plaine Avenue………………………………………………....	26
Sunnyside Avenue…………………………………………………..	28
Hubbard Street………………………………………………………	30
Moody Avenue……………………………………………………….	32
Laramie Avenue……………………………………………………..	34

Duets for One Alto and One Tenor:

Fairbanks Court……………………………………………………...	38
Armitage Avenue…………………………………………………….	40
Ozark Avenue………………………………………………………...	42
Peterson Avenue…………………………………………………….	44
Wilson Avenue……………………………………………………….	46
Belle Plaine Avenue………………………………………………....	48
Sunnyside Avenue…………………………………………………..	50
Hubbard Street………………………………………………………	52
Moody Avenue……………………………………………………….	54
Laramie Avenue……………………………………………………..	56
About the Author…………………………………………………….	60

©2010 Greg Fishman
All rights reserved. International copyright secured.

PREFACE

I've always been a huge fan of the two-saxophone format. Al Cohn & Zoot Sims, Sonny Stitt & Gene Ammons, Dexter Gordon & Wardell Gray, Lee Konitz & Warne Marsh, and Johnny Griffin & Eddie "Lockjaw" Davis have all had a profound influence on both my playing and writing. I love the excitement generated by the interaction between the two saxophonists and their rhythm sections.

As a young player, hearing those famous two-saxophone groups was very inspiring. I would transcribe the arrangements and play right along with the records. Later, when I started playing in jazz clubs, I formed my own two-tenor group. It was always fun and exciting, and the interplay between the two saxophones was a constant source of new musical ideas.

I learned so much on the bandstand playing in this format that I decided to create a series of jazz duet books that would give students an opportunity to experience the excitement of playing professional-level sax duets with a great rhythm section.

This book offers maximum flexibility, giving saxophonists the choice of playing with two altos, two tenors or alto and tenor. A unique feature of this book is that both alto and tenor saxophonists read the same written part while the rhythm section transposes to accommodate the saxophonists.

The three play-along CDs included with this book feature four different versions of each duet. The first track features both saxophones plus the rhythm section; the second track features the second saxophone part plus the rhythm section; the third track features the first saxophone part plus the rhythm section; the fourth track features the rhythm section only, with extra choruses for soloing. These extra choruses allow the saxophonists to musically communicate with each other by trading choruses or phrases during the solo section of the play-along tracks.

This book will help you develop your ear and mind so that you can become adept at expressing yourself through your own improvisations. I hope you enjoy it!

— Greg Fishman

PERSONNEL CREDITS

Greg Fishman – Alto and Tenor Saxophone

Saxophonist, recording artist and educator Greg Fishman has performed with The Woody Herman Band, Louis Bellson, Lou Levy, Slide Hampton, Conte Candoli, Phil Woods, Don Menza, Clark Terry, Eddie Higgins, Harry Allen and Jackie & Roy. He has performed at jazz festivals and clubs nationally and internationally, including the Monterey Jazz Festival, the North Sea Jazz Festival in the Netherlands, and the Fujitsu – Concord Jazz festival in Japan. Greg earned his master's degree in Jazz Pedagogy at Northwestern University. He earned his bachelor's degree in Jazz Studies at DePaul University. Greg is the author of three Stan Getz transcription books (published by Hal Leonard) as well as *Jazz Saxophone Etudes Vols. 1 - 3, Jazz Saxophone Duets Vols. 1 – 3, Jazz Phrasing for Beginners, Jazz Guitar Etudes, Jazz Trumpet Duets,* and *Tasting Harmony* (published by Greg Fishman Jazz Studios).

Web site: www.gregfishman.com
Web site: www.gregfishmanjazzstudios.com
E-mail: greg@gregfishmanjazzstudios.com

Mark Colby – Tenor Saxophone (2nd Saxophone)

Saxophonist, recording artist and educator Mark Colby has performed and/or recorded with Gerry Mulligan, Frank Sinatra, Clark Terry, Maynard Ferguson, Jaco Pastorius, Chuck Mangione, Ira Sullivan, Phil Woods, Charlie Haden, and Bob James. He has also released critically acclaimed albums as a leader, and records for Origin Records and Hallway Records. He has been a jazz faculty member at DePaul University since 1983, and Elmhurst College since 1998. As a representative of Selmer saxophones and Vandoren Reeds, he performs as a guest soloist and clinician/adjudicator at high schools and colleges nationwide.

Web site: www.markcolby.com
E-mail: mark.colby@sbcglobal.net

Dennis Luxion – Piano

Pianist, recording artist and educator Dennis Luxion toured and recorded with Chet Baker, and has performed with Curtis Fuller, Von Freeman, Lee Konitz, Ira Sullivan, Woody Shaw, Archie Shepp, and Toots Thielmans. He studied music at the University of Illinois, DePaul University, Illinois Benedictine University, and the Royal Conservatory of Music in Liege, Belgium. He currently teaches jazz piano at Columbia College in Chicago.

E-mail: deluxmusic@hotmail.com

Eric Hochberg – Bass

Bassist, recording artist and producer Eric Hochberg has performed and/or recorded with such artists as Cannonball Adderley, Pharoah Sanders, Mark Murphy, Pat Metheny, Lyle Mays, Bob Mintzer, Dave Liebman, Bob Sheppard, and Randy Brecker. He is the producer of several acclaimed albums on the Blue Note and Emarcy/Sony Japan labels. He studied music at Indiana University and earned his degree in communications from Northwestern University.

Web site: www.erichochbergmusic.com
E-mail: ehochberg@sbcglobal.net

Phil Gratteau – Drums

Drummer, recording artist and educator Phil Gratteau received his bachelor's degree in Music Education at the University of Illinois, and his master's degree in Jazz Pedagogy at Northwestern University. He has performed and/or recorded with Joe Henderson, Richie Cole, Kevin Mahogany, Marian McPartland, Frank Mantooth, Dorothy Donegan, and Herb Ellis. He has taught at the American Conservatory of Music, and currently teaches at North Park University, and the Chicago College of Performing Arts at Roosevelt University.

E-mail: pgratteau@hotmail.com

PRODUCTION CREDITS

Composed and arranged by: Greg Fishman
Published by: Greg Fishman Jazz Studios, Evanston, Illinois
Edited by: Judy Roberts
Music editor: Dennis Luxion
Proofreading: Paul Maslin, David Kromelow
Cover photo: Jos. L. Knaepen
Graphic design: Russ Paladino
Book printing: Omnigraphix, Morton Grove, Illinois
CD printing: Universal Recording Supplies, Inc.
Music engraving: Greg Fishman
Recorded at: Studiomedia, Evanston, Illinois
Engineered, mixed and mastered by Scott Steinman

Greg Fishman is a Rico artist and plays Rico reeds exclusively.

SUGGESTED USE OF THIS BOOK AND CD SET

THE IDIOMATIC CONCEPT

This duet book was written with the idiomatic tendencies of the saxophone in mind. While some technical challenges are present, these duets will feel comfortable and natural for all saxophone players.

If you've ever tried playing an alto solo transposed for tenor (or vice-versa), you know that the transposed version of the solo never seems to "lay right" on the non-native horn. This is because all of the fingerings of the notes have changed. In addition to the fingering changes, some notes will be out of the normal range of the saxophone. As a result, portions of some phrases need to be transposed up or down an octave. This transposition disrupts the natural flow of the original melodic line.

My solution for this problem is to have the both the alto and tenor saxophonists read the same written part and have the rhythm section transpose to accommodate the saxophonists.

THE ALTO & TENOR

One of my goals for this book was to ensure maximum flexibility for all players. I needed to find a way in which I could employ the idiomatic concept discussed above, yet give saxophonists the option to play the duets with the combination of one alto and one tenor, as well as the more common two-alto or two-tenor approach.

My solution for this challenge was to write duets in which the first sax part favors the upper range of the instrument. This means that what was originally a high "F" in the tenor part will now be a "C" two ledger lines above the staff when transposed for alto. This minimizes the negative effects of playing a transposed part, because all notes will be in a comfortable range of the horn, and there's no need to change octaves to accommodate the written music.

On pages 38 through 58, the two staves of the duets are in two different key signatures. The top staff is the alto part and the bottom staff is the tenor part. In most cases, the alto part has been transposed down a fourth from the same written parts that appear in the first half of the book. The tenor part is the same as it was in the first half of the book. However, there are two exceptions: "Sunnyside Avenue" and "Moody Avenue" sounded better when I transposed the second sax part up a fourth, rather than lowering the first sax part.

For ease of reading, the words "Alto" and "Tenor," as well as the abbreviations "A" for alto and "T" for tenor have been used at the left side of each stave for the alto/tenor duet section of this book.

USING THE CDs

There are three CDs included with this book:

Eb Alto Saxophone Version – Use this disc to play the duets with two altos or two baritones. The duets corresponding with this CD start on page 16.

Bb Tenor Saxophone Version – Use this disc to play the duets with two tenors or two sopranos. The duets corresponding with this CD start on page 16.

Alto & Tenor Version – Use this disc to play the duets with alto playing the first part (top staff) and tenor playing the second part (bottom staff). The duets corresponding to this CD start on page 38.

SELECTING THE CD TRACKS

In order to provide the player with multiple practice options, I've included four different recorded versions of each duet.

Each CD has forty-one tracks. Tracks 1 – 40 contain four different versions of each of the ten duets. Track 41 is a tuning track with a piano playing concert A and concert Bb.

HOW TO USE THE FOUR CORRESPONDING CD TRACKS

The first CD track includes both saxophone parts plus the rhythm section. The duet is played once through, going to the final ending.

Use this track to become familiar with the way in which the two sax parts fit together. You can play either the first or second sax part along with this track.

The second CD track features the second saxophone part plus the rhythm section. It's identical to the first track, but with the first sax part muted. This track can be used two ways:

1. Play the first sax part along with the CD so that you can hear both parts of the duet simultaneously, even if you don't have another saxophonist available to play the duet "live."

2. Play the second sax part along with the CD, matching the recorded sax for tone, style, articulation, etc.

The third track features the first saxophone part plus the rhythm section. It's identical to the first track, but with the second sax part muted. This track can be used two ways:

1. Play the second sax part along with the CD so that you can hear both parts of the duet simultaneously, even if you don't have another saxophonist available to play the duet "live."

2. Play the first sax part along with the CD, matching the recorded sax for tone, style, articulation, etc.

The fourth track is played with the rhythm section only, and includes extra choruses for soloing. Use this track to play the duet with another saxophonist present, as well as for soloing over the chord changes. After playing once through the melody, improvise over the chord progressions for the specified number of choruses before playing the melody to conclude the piece on the final chorus of the track.

When playing along with the fourth track, the duets use this format:

Melody / 4 Solo Choruses / Melody

This means that after you've played the melody, solo for the number of choruses indicated between the forward slash marks. In the example above, there are four solo choruses before the final melody chorus. If there are two players present, you can each play two solo choruses and then play the melody again, or you can trade choruses or eight-bar phrases four times through the form before playing the melody again.

CD TRACK SUMMARY

If you'd like to play through the entire book with one particular instrumentation format, use the table below to determine the proper tracks to program on your CD player.

CD INSTRUMENTATION	CD Track Numbers									
Saxes 1 & 2 + Rhythm Section	1	5	9	13	17	21	25	29	33	37
Sax 2 + Rhythm Section	2	6	10	14	18	22	26	30	34	38
Sax 1 + Rhythm Section	3	7	11	15	19	23	27	31	35	39
Rhythm Section Only	4	8	12	16	20	24	28	32	36	40

ABOUT THE MUSIC

TEMPOS

The tempos for some of the duets may be faster than those to which the advancing player is accustomed. However, these tempos are actually quite conservative by professional standards.

Each duet was written to be played at the marked tempo. If you're not comfortable playing at these high speeds, set your metronome at half the marked tempo and play through the duet, circling any passages that pose a technical challenge. Practice the circled areas until you can play them smoothly and accurately.

As your technique improves, increase the metronome setting one click at a time, and slowly work your way up to the marked tempo. Your goal should be to play the entire duet at the marked tempo with no mistakes, and with the correct style and articulation.

DYNAMICS

The duets have a natural dynamic balance between the two saxophone parts. Use *forte* as a general starting point for the dynamic level of the duets, but let your ear be your guide for when to play slightly louder or softer. Listen carefully to the play-along CDs for an example of the subtle dynamic variations in the individual lines as well as the dynamic balance between the two saxophone parts.

ADDITIONAL CHORD CHANGES

"Wilson Avenue" features one extra chord change in the twelfth measure. The extra chord is notated in parenthesis between the staves. It is played only on the first and last chorus of the accompanying CD track. When soloing, use the chords above the first sax part.

COURTESY ACCIDENTALS

Since the tempos are on the fast side and the duets have many accidentals, I've included courtesy accidentals to improve the readability of the parts.

OUTLINING THE GOALS FOR THREE LEVELS

This book is designed to work well for three levels of players: intermediate, advanced and professional. Below, I've outlined three different approaches for practicing the duets.

INTERMEDIATE LEVEL

The intermediate level player usually has several years of experience playing jazz in big bands or combos, has memorized chords and scales, and is starting to get comfortable with the concept of improvisation.

For the intermediate player, this book will provide a good model of jazz phrasing and logical development of musical ideas, as well as some technical challenges. It will also sharpen sight reading skills.

The basic goal of the intermediate player is to emulate the saxophone playing on the recorded examples. Close attention should be paid to all stylistic aspects as demonstrated on the play-along CDs, including articulation, time-feel, phrasing, etc.

If you're an intermediate player and you'd like to move up to the next playing level, you should practice arpeggiating the chords for each duet from the root up to the seventh. The root of the chord is especially important for ear training purposes. I suggest playing the roots of each chord along with the CD.

Once you've played through the duets like this a few times, try to accurately sing the bass-note pitches with the different versions of the play-along tracks. This will help train your ear to hear the relationship between the melodies of the duets and the root movement of the chords. Once these goals are accomplished, you're ready to move on to the advanced level.

ADVANCED LEVEL

The goal for the advanced player is to understand the way in which each phrase is developed, how the notes in the phrases relate to each chord, and how both sax parts in the duet progress logically from one idea to the next.

As an advanced player, you should be adept at arpeggiating the chords from the root up to the thirteenth. You should also practice playing isolated notes in each chord up to tempo. For example, you should be able to play all of the thirds, fifths, sevenths, ninths, elevenths and thirteenths of each chord accurately and in time with the rhythm section.

When soloing over the rhythm section tracks, try to make your improvised choruses sound like they're in the same general style as the opening chorus, using some of the musical phrases in your part of the duet as a point of departure for your own improvisation.

To prepare for the next level, memorize the chord progressions as well as both the first and second sax parts of the duets. I also suggest choosing your favorite phrases or licks from each duet, and practicing them in all twelve keys, up to tempo. Once you've achieved these goals, you're ready to move on to the professional level.

PROFESSIONAL LEVEL

By the time you've reached this level, you're an extremely accomplished player, probably a professional musician and/or educator, and are still totally absorbed and inspired, as I am, by this great art form.

Study the duets from an analytical and compositional standpoint. I recommend doing a measure-by-measure analysis of each duet. Determine what type of writing is being used to create a particular effect. For example, parallel thirds always sound pleasing to the ear and produce a uniform rhythmic effect. On the other hand, sometimes a counter-melody in the second sax part will nicely offset the lead-line in the first sax part.

In some situations, the musical focus might be on a particularly dissonant interval, such as a minor second or major seventh. Analyze each interval produced by the two sax parts and note the effect they have on the feeling of tension or release throughout the duets. Once you've done some analysis, write your own duets using these various compositional devices.

MORE RESOURCES AVAILABLE ONLINE

If you'd like to read more about my concepts on jazz improvisation, please visit my educational Web site at: www.gregfishmanjazzstudios.com. You'll find downloadable articles on theory and ear-training, as well as a variety of licks and useful practice tips.

CLINICS, MASTERCLASSES AND CONCERT PERFORMANCES

For information regarding clinics, masterclasses and concert bookings in the U.S. and internationally, contact:

Greg Fishman
Greg Fishman Jazz Studios
824 Custer Avenue
Evanston, Illinois 60202
(847)334-3634

Web site: www.gregfishmanjazzstudios.com
E-mail: greg@gregfishmanjazzstudios.com

PRIVATE LESSONS

Lessons include the following: study of the saxophone, jazz improvisation, transcription, ear-training, repertoire, memorization techniques, theory, and chord substitution. Students who study with me at my Chicago-area studio receive a CD recording of each lesson.

LESSONS BY E-MAIL

I have developed an effective e-mail lesson program customized for each student's unique needs. Students record themselves playing for approximately ten minutes and send that recording to me as an e-mail attachment. I listen to the recording and provide a live running commentary on their playing. This provides the student with direct, constructive and professional feedback on their performance.

In addition to the commentary, the e-mail lessons also include licks and patterns, as well as assignments designed to improve tone, technique, ear-training, theory, vocabulary, etc.

For further details on E-mail lessons, visit: www.gregfishmanjazzstudios.com.

Style & Analysis

WRITING STYLES

Below are examples of some of the different writing styles used throughout this book. These duets were written in a postbop jazz style, and I've adapted the writing styles to fit the idiom. At times, I've used a liberal interpretation of some of the strict rules usually associated with these writing styles. It should be noted that the duets sometimes employ a particular writing style for only a few beats or measures at a time.

Imitation

Imitation is a device in which a theme is stated in one voice and repeated in a different voice. In the example below, the upper voice states a theme in measures one and three, and the lower voice imitates that theme in measures two and four.

"Wilson Avenue," mm. 1-4

Parallel Motion

With parallel motion, the voices move in the same direction by the same interval. In the example below, I've used parallel motion in 3rds.

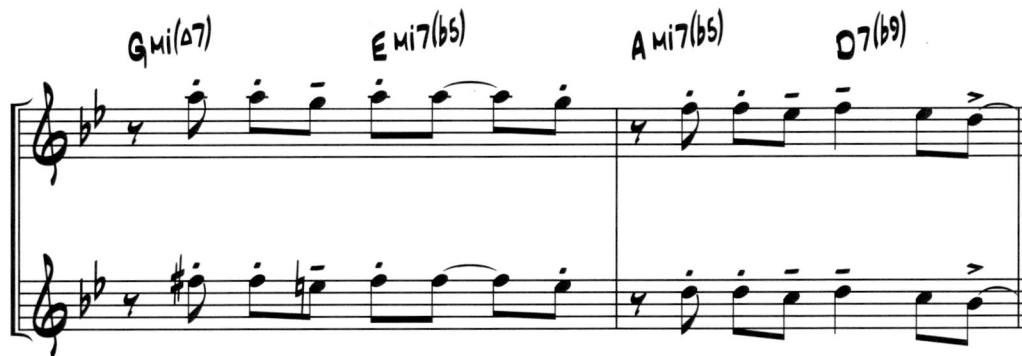

"Armitage Avenue," mm.5-6

Contrary Motion

With contrary motion, the voices move in opposite directions by any interval.

"Belle Plaine Avenue," mm. 19

Oblique Motion

With oblique motion, one voice moves up or down while the other voice stays on the same pitch.

"Fairbanks Court," mm. 36

Counterpoint

Counterpoint involves the use of two or more independent, simultaneous melodies. The intervals resulting from the independent lines imply the song's harmonic structure.

"Peterson Avenue," mm.1-4

DETAILED OVERVIEW OF THE DUETS

Title	Tempo	Form	Length of Form	Saxophone Key Signature	Page Number for Two Altos or Two Tenors	Page Number for Alto and Tenor	CD Track Numbers
Fairbanks Court	♩ = 208	ABAC	32 Bars	G Major	16	38	1 – 4
Armitage Avenue	♩ = 132	AABA	32 Bars	G Minor	18	40	5 – 8
Ozark Avenue	♩ = 192	AABA	40 Bars	D Major	20	42	9 – 12
Peterson Avenue	♩ = 180	ABA	24 Bars	F Minor	22	44	13 – 16
Wilson Avenue	♩ = 172	AA^{1}BA^2	36 Bars	Bb Major	24	46	17 – 20
Belle Plaine Ave.	♩ = 164	ABAB	48 Bars	Eb Major	26	48	21 – 24
Sunnyside Avenue	♩ = 148	ABAC	34 Bars	G Major	28	50	25 – 28
Hubbard Street	♩ = 192	BLUES	24 Bars	F Major	30	52	29 – 32
Moody Avenue	♩ = 80	ABAB^1	32 Bars	G Major	32	54	33 – 36
Laramie Avenue	♩ = 212	AABA^1	34 Bars	D Major	34	56	37 – 40

©2010 Greg Fishman Jazz Studios
All Rights Reserved. International Copyright Secured.

CD TRACK #5 (SAXES 1 & 2 + RHYTHM SECTION)
CD TRACK #6 (SAX 2 + RHYTHM SECTION)
CD TRACK #7 (SAX 1 + RHYTHM SECTION)
CD TRACK #8 (RHYTHM SECTION ONLY)

COUNT OFF: 2 BARS (6 CLICKS)

PLAY 4X (MELODY / 2 SOLO CHORUSES / MELODY)

GREG FISHMAN

Armitage Avenue

CD TRACK #13 (SAXES 1 & 2 + RHYTHM SECTION)
CD TRACK #14 (SAX 2 + RHYTHM SECTION)
CD TRACK #15 (SAX 1 + RHYTHM SECTION)
CD TRACK #16 (RHYTHM SECTION ONLY)

COUNT OFF: 1 BAR (5 CLICKS)

PLAY 6X (MELODY / 4 SOLO CHORUSES / MELODY)

Peterson Avenue

Greg Fishman

©2010 Greg Fishman Jazz Studios
All Rights Reserved. International Copyright Secured.

CD TRACK #21 (SAXES 1 & 2 + RHYTHM SECTION)
CD TRACK #22 (SAX 2 + RHYTHM SECTION)
CD TRACK #23 (SAX 1 + RHYTHM SECTION)
CD TRACK #24 (RHYTHM SECTION ONLY)

COUNT OFF: 4 BARS (8 CLICKS)

PLAY 4X (MELODY / 2 SOLO CHORUSES / MELODY)

Greg Fishman

Belle Plaine Avenue

CD TRACK #25 (SAXES 1 & 2 + RHYTHM SECTION)
CD TRACK #26 (SAX 2 + RHYTHM SECTION)
CD TRACK #27 (SAX 1 + RHYTHM SECTION)
CD TRACK #28 (RHYTHM SECTION ONLY)

COUNT OFF: 2 BARS (6 CLICKS)

PLAY 4X (MELODY / 2 SOLO CHORUSES / MELODY)

Sunnyside Avenue

Greg Fishman

©2010 Greg Fishman Jazz Studios
All Rights Reserved. International Copyright Secured.

CD TRACK #29 (SAXES 1 & 2 + RHYTHM SECTION)
CD TRACK #30 (SAX 2 + RHYTHM SECTION)
CD TRACK #31 (SAX 1 + RHYTHM SECTION)
CD TRACK #32 (RHYTHM SECTION ONLY)

COUNT OFF: 2 BARS (6 CLICKS)

PLAY 6X (MELODY / 4 SOLO CHORUSES / MELODY)

Hubbard Street

GREG FISHMAN

©2010 Greg Fishman Jazz Studios
All Rights Reserved. International Copyright Secured.

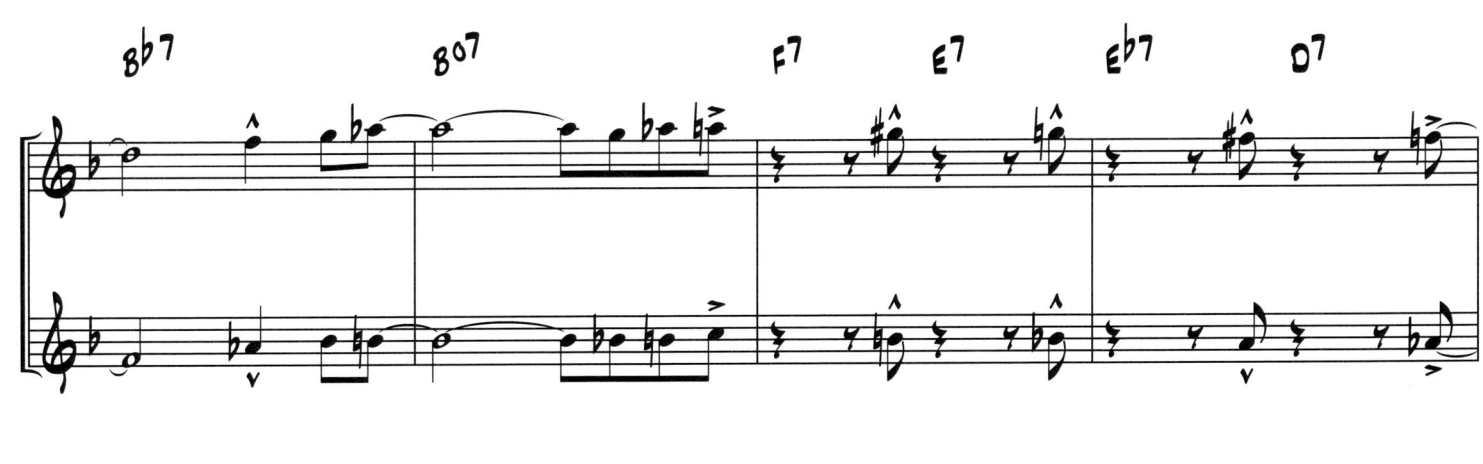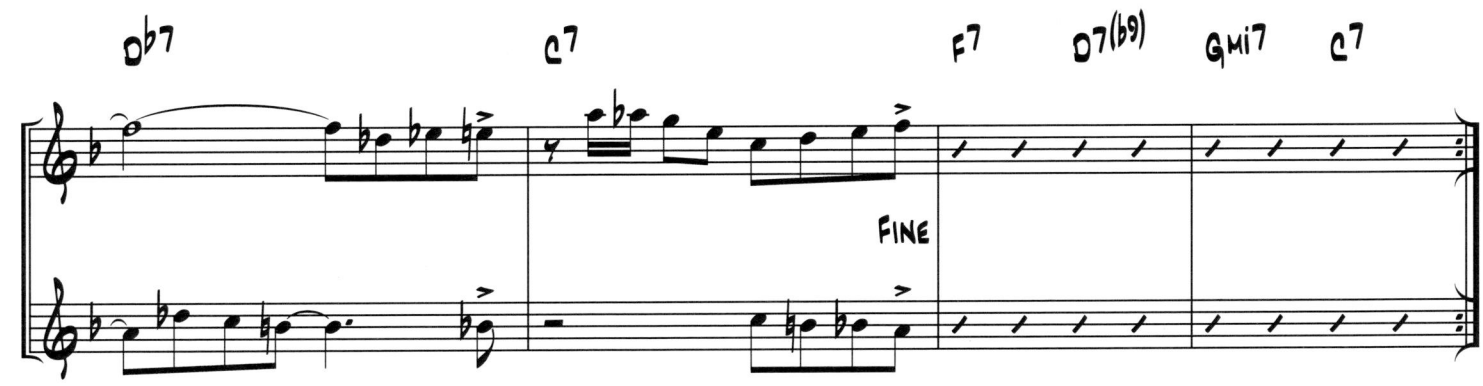

CD TRACK #33 (SAXES 1 & 2 + RHYTHM SECTION)
CD TRACK #34 (SAX 2 + RHYTHM SECTION)
CD TRACK #35 (SAX 1 + RHYTHM SECTION)
CD TRACK #36 (RHYTHM SECTION ONLY)

COUNT OFF: 1 BAR (4 CLICKS)

PLAY 3X (MELODY / 1 SOLO CHORUS / MELODY)

GREG FISHMAN

Moody Avenue

©2010 Greg Fishman Jazz Studios
All Rights Reserved. International Copyright Secured.

CD TRACK #37 (SAXES 1 & 2 + RHYTHM SECTION)
CD TRACK #38 (SAX 2 + RHYTHM SECTION)
CD TRACK #39 (SAX 1 + RHYTHM SECTION)
CD TRACK #40 (RHYTHM SECTION ONLY)

COUNT OFF: 2 BARS (6 CLICKS)

PLAY 6X (MELODY / 4 SOLO CHORUSES / MELODY)

GREG FISHMAN

Laramie Avenue

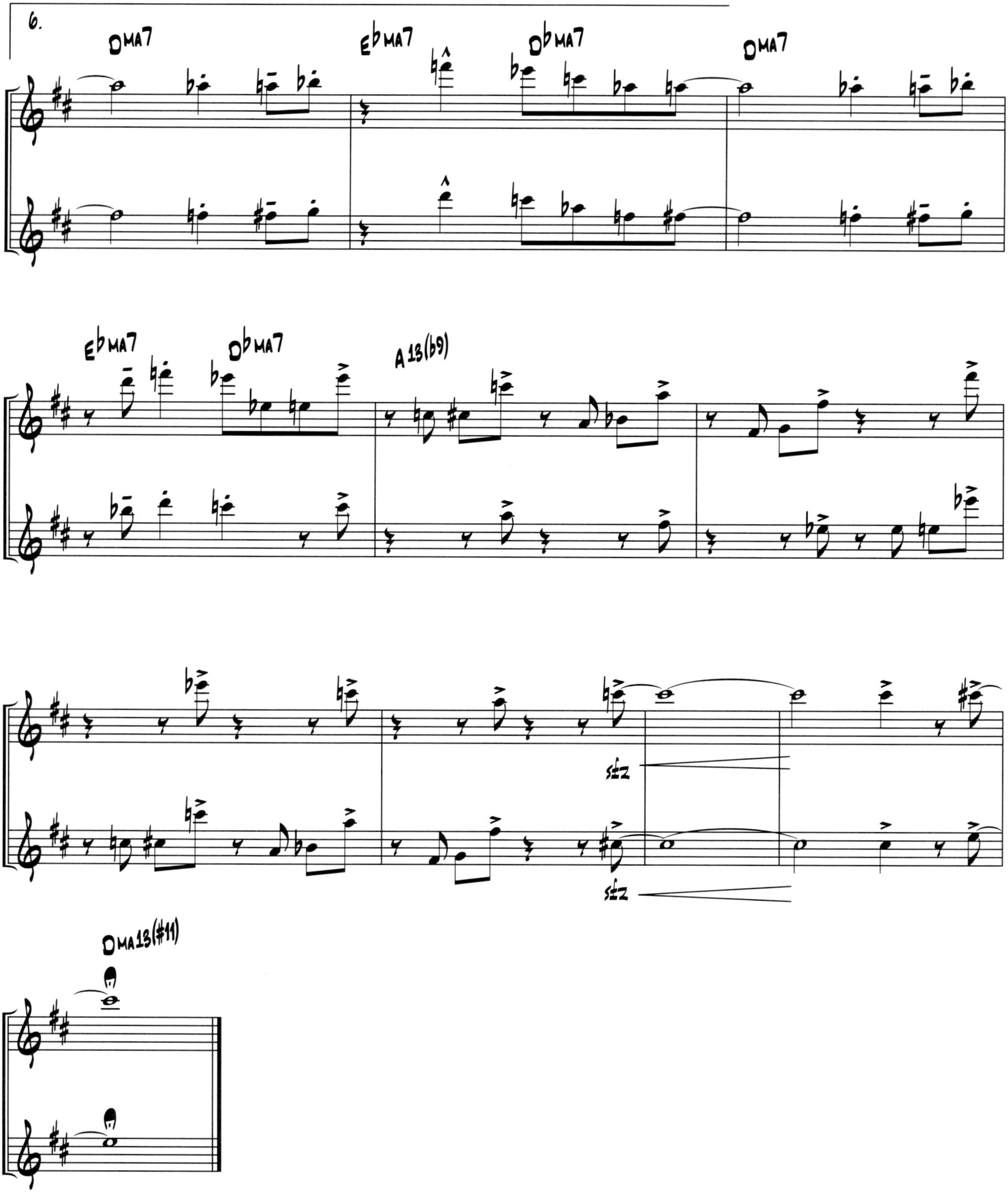
6.
DMA7
E♭MA7
D♭MA7
DMA7
E♭MA7
D♭MA7
A13(♭9)
sfz
sfz
DMA13(#11)

Jazz Saxophone Duets
Volume 2
by Greg Fishman

Duets for One Alto and One Tenor:

Fairbanks Court…	38
Armitage Avenue…	40
Ozark Avenue…	42
Peterson Avenue…	44
Wilson Avenue…	46
Belle Plaine Avenue…	48
Sunnyside Avenue…	50
Hubbard Street…	52
Moody Avenue…	54
Laramie Avenue…	56

CD TRACK #1 (SAXES 1 & 2 + RHYTHM SECTION)
CD TRACK #2 (SAX 2 + RHYTHM SECTION)
CD TRACK #3 (SAX 1 + RHYTHM SECTION)
CD TRACK #4 (RHYTHM SECTION ONLY)

COUNT OFF: 2 BARS (6 CLICKS)

PLAY 6X (MELODY / 4 SOLO CHORUSES / MELODY)

Greg Fishman

Fairbanks Court

©2010 Greg Fishman Jazz Studios
All Rights Reserved. International Copyright Secured.

CD TRACK #2 (SAXES 1 & 2 + RHYTHM SECTION)
CD TRACK #3 (SAX 2 + RHYTHM SECTION)
CD TRACK #4 (SAX 1 + RHYTHM SECTION)
CD TRACK #5 (RHYTHM SECTION ONLY)

COUNT OFF: 2 BARS (6 CLICKS)

PLAY 4X (MELODY / 2 SOLO CHORUSES / MELODY)

Greg Fishman

Armitage Avenue

CD TRACK #13 (SAXES 1 & 2 + RHYTHM SECTION)
CD TRACK #14 (SAX 2 + RHYTHM SECTION)
CD TRACK #15 (SAX 1 + RHYTHM SECTION)
CD TRACK #16 (RHYTHM SECTION ONLY)

COUNT OFF: 1 BAR (5 CLICKS)

PLAY 6X (MELODY / 4 SOLO CHORUSES / MELODY)

Greg Fishman

Peterson Avenue

CD TRACK #17 (SAXES 1 & 2 + RHYTHM SECTION)
CD TRACK #18 (SAX 2 + RHYTHM SECTION)
CD TRACK #19 (SAX 1 + RHYTHM SECTION)
CD TRACK #20 (RHYTHM SECTION ONLY)

COUNT OFF: 2 BARS (6 CLICKS)

PLAY 6X (MELODY / 4 SOLO CHORUSES / MELODY)

GREG FISHMAN

Wilson Avenue

CD TRACK #25 (SAXES 1 & 2 + RHYTHM SECTION)
CD TRACK #26 (SAX 2 + RHYTHM SECTION)
CD TRACK #27 (SAX 1 + RHYTHM SECTION)
CD TRACK #28 (RHYTHM SECTION ONLY)

COUNT OFF: 2 BARS (6 CLICKS)

PLAY 4X (MELODY / 2 SOLO CHORUSES / MELODY)

Greg Fishman

Sunnyside Avenue

CD TRACK #29 (SAXES 1 & 2 + RHYTHM SECTION)
CD TRACK #30 (SAX 2 + RHYTHM SECTION)
CD TRACK #31 (SAX 1 + RHYTHM SECTION)
CD TRACK #32 (RHYTHM SECTION ONLY)

COUNT OFF: 2 BARS (6 CLICKS)

PLAY 6X (MELODY / 4 SOLO CHORUSES / MELODY)

Greg Fishman

Hubbard Street

CD TRACK #33 (SAXES 1 & 2 + RHYTHM SECTION)
CD TRACK #34 (SAX 2 + RHYTHM SECTION)
CD TRACK #35 (SAX 1 + RHYTHM SECTION)
CD TRACK #36 (RHYTHM SECTION ONLY)

COUNT OFF: 1 BAR (4 CLICKS)

PLAY 3X (MELODY / 1 SOLO CHORUS / MELODY)

Greg Fishman

Moody Avenue

©2010 Greg Fishman Jazz Studios
All Rights Reserved. International Copyright Secured.

CD TRACK #37 (SAXES 1 & 2 + RHYTHM SECTION)
CD TRACK #38 (SAX 2 + RHYTHM SECTION)
CD TRACK #39 (SAX 1 + RHYTHM SECTION)
CD TRACK #40 (RHYTHM SECTION ONLY)

Greg Fishman

Laramie Avenue

COUNT OFF: 2 BARS (6 CLICKS)

PLAY 6X (MELODY / 4 SOLO CHORUSES / MELODY)

©2010 Greg Fishman Jazz Studios
All Rights Reserved. International Copyright Secured.

6.

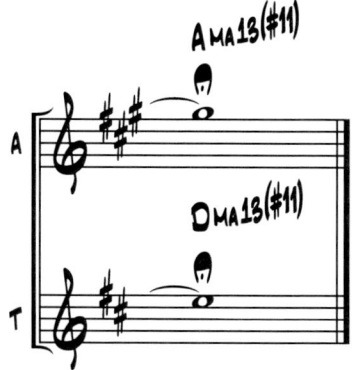

THESE BOOKS WILL CHANGE THE WAY YOU LEARN THE LANGUAGE OF JAZZ

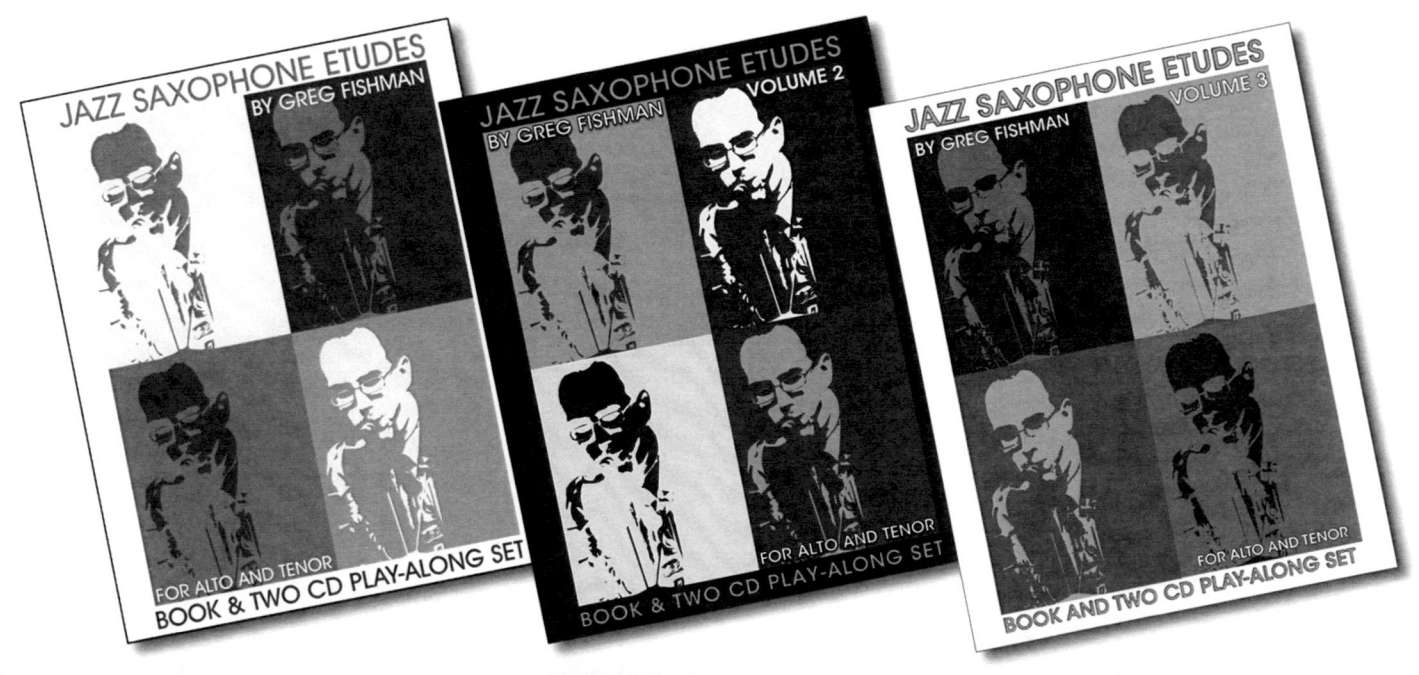

Jazz Saxophone Etudes **Vol 1** • Jazz Saxophone Etudes **Vol 2** • Jazz Saxophone Etudes **Vol 3**

"A powerful sight reading, ear training, swinging, improvising jazz tool. Perfect for the student of jazz."
— **Michael Brecker**

"Greg Fishman dares to explore new musical heights. Every lesson in Greg's books is a must for all musicians, and this latest book is no exception. Greg, you've done a beautiful, musical thing again!"
— **James Moody**

"These well-crafted pieces clearly and authentically demonstrate the building blocks of bebop/hardbop melody, phrasing and rhythm. Greg's books are now a part of the jazz curriculum of the University of Miami."
— **Gary Keller**
Professor of Saxophone, University of Miami

"Greg's etudes are fun-to-play gems. Great for demonstrating phrasing and vocabulary."
— **Bob Sheppard**

"These etudes are wonderfully written and conceived. They really capture the essence of what students need to learn about jazz vocabulary. This is a great tool for teaching and learning for all ages."
— **Mark Colby**

To order by phone, mail or online:
PM Woodwind - 822 Custer Ave, Evanston, IL 60202 - (847) 869-7049
www.gregfishmanjazzstudios.com

About the Author

Saxophonist and flutist Greg Fishman is an accomplished performer, recording artist, author, teacher and clinician. Born in Chicago in 1967, he began playing professionally at age fourteen. Greg graduated from DePaul University in Chicago with a degree in Jazz Performance, and earned a Masters Degree in Jazz Pedagogy from Northwestern University. He is among the foremost experts on the music of Stan Getz and is the author of three Getz transcription books published by Hal Leonard. His self-published books, *Jazz Saxophone Etudes, Volumes 1 – 3*, *Jazz Saxophone Duets, Volumes 1 – 3*, *Jazz Phrasing for Beginners*, *Jazz Guitar Etudes*, *Jazz Trumpet Duets* and *Tasting Harmony* are in circulation worldwide and have been endorsed by top educators and jazz performers, including Michael Brecker, Jerry Coker and Phil Woods.

Greg is a contributing author of jazz theory articles for Jazz Improv magazine, JAZZed, Chicago Jazz Magazine, IAJE Jazz Educators Journal, and was featured on the cover of *Saxophone Journal*, for whom he also writes. He is the author of the liner notes for the Verve reissue of the Getz recording *The Steamer*.

Greg has toured and performed worldwide with his own group, and with such artists as Phil Woods, the Woody Herman Band, Louis Bellson, Slide Hampton, Conte Candoli, Lou Levy, Clark Terry, Jackie and Roy, Don Menza, Ira Sullivan, Judy Roberts, Jeremy Monteiro, Jimmy Heath, Lou Donaldson, Harry Allen, Jeff Hamilton, Eddie Higgins, and Benny Golson.

Greg is the co-founder, along with Brazilian guitarist/vocalist, Paulinho Garcia, of the award-winning duo, "Two for Brazil." They perform worldwide, and have recorded five CDs. Greg's current discography features additional jazz releases in the U.S., Singapore, and Japan.

In addition to clubs and concerts in the U.S., Greg has been featured at the Concord-Fujitsu jazz festival in Japan, the NorthSea Jazz Festival in the Netherlands, and in numerous concerts in Hong Kong, Bangkok, Singapore, China and Israel.

Greg teaches jazz master classes and college workshops nationally and internationally, and is on the faculty of the Jamey Aebersold Summer Jazz Workshop.

When not on tour, Greg is based in the Chicago area where he performs locally and teaches at Greg Fishman Jazz Studios.

Greg Fishman is a Rico artist and plays Rico reeds exclusively.

"...His solos are shrewdly conceived yet delivered with apparent ease and elegance. He develops harmonies that sometimes startle the ear as he forges lines that take unexpected twists and turns..."
— Chicago Tribune

"Greg Fishman dares to explore new musical heights. Every lesson in Greg's books is a must for all musicians, and this latest book is no exception. Greg, you've done a beautiful, musical thing again!"
— James Moody